50 Clean Eating Dishes

By: Kelly Johnson

Table of Contents

- Classic Acai Bowl
- Peanut Butter Banana Oat Bowl
- Berry Almond Chia Pudding Bowl
- Greek Yogurt and Honey Granola Bowl
- Quinoa and Fresh Fruit Bowl
- Green Detox Smoothie Bowl
- Apple Cinnamon Oatmeal Bowl
- Tropical Mango Coconut Bowl
- Protein-Packed Egg and Avocado Bowl
- Choco-Banana Smoothie Bowl
- Spiced Pumpkin Oatmeal Bowl
- Matcha and Coconut Yogurt Bowl
- Blueberry Walnut Overnight Oats Bowl
- Avocado and Smoked Salmon Quinoa Bowl
- Chia and Flaxseed Superfood Bowl
- Sweet Potato and Almond Butter Bowl
- Strawberry and Cacao Nib Yogurt Bowl
- Peanut Butter Chocolate Oatmeal Bowl
- Spiced Pear and Pecan Quinoa Bowl
- Mediterranean Feta and Chickpea Bowl
- Carrot Cake Overnight Oats Bowl
- Vanilla Bean and Berry Chia Bowl
- Dragon Fruit and Pineapple Bowl
- Scrambled Tofu and Avocado Bowl
- Almond Joy Smoothie Bowl
- Honeydew and Kiwi Yogurt Bowl
- High-Protein Cottage Cheese Bowl
- Cinnamon Apple Quinoa Porridge Bowl
- Chocolate Hazelnut Smoothie Bowl
- Roasted Chickpea and Spinach Bowl
- Blackberry and Mint Greek Yogurt Bowl
- Spicy Black Bean and Avocado Bowl
- Caramelized Banana and Walnut Oat Bowl
- Lemon Poppy Seed Chia Pudding Bowl
- Maple Pecan Overnight Oats Bowl

- Spiced Chai Quinoa Bowl
- Raspberry and Dark Chocolate Yogurt Bowl
- Baked Oatmeal Blueberry Bowl
- Fig and Almond Butter Smoothie Bowl
- Banana Nut Muffin Oatmeal Bowl
- Hemp and Coconut Yogurt Bowl
- Golden Turmeric Chia Pudding Bowl
- Pear and Cinnamon Greek Yogurt Bowl
- Pomegranate and Pistachio Bowl
- Dark Cherry Almond Butter Bowl
- Pumpkin Spice Smoothie Bowl
- Sweet and Savory Avocado Egg Bowl
- Cashew Butter and Cacao Smoothie Bowl
- Gingerbread Oatmeal Bowl
- Mocha Banana Protein Bowl

Classic Açaí Bowl

Ingredients:

- 1 frozen açaí packet
- 1 banana
- ½ cup frozen mixed berries
- ½ cup almond milk
- 1 teaspoon honey (optional)
- ¼ cup granola
- Fresh fruit, coconut flakes, and chia seeds for topping

Instructions:

1. Blend açaí, banana, frozen berries, and almond milk until smooth.
2. Pour into a bowl and top with granola, fresh fruit, coconut flakes, and chia seeds.

Peanut Butter Banana Oat Bowl

Ingredients:

- ½ cup rolled oats
- 1 cup almond milk
- 1 banana, sliced
- 1 tablespoon peanut butter
- 1 teaspoon chia seeds
- 1 teaspoon honey

Instructions:

1. Cook oats in almond milk until creamy.
2. Top with banana slices, peanut butter, chia seeds, and honey.

Berry Almond Chia Pudding Bowl

Ingredients:

- ¼ cup chia seeds
- 1 cup almond milk
- 1 teaspoon vanilla extract
- 1 tablespoon honey
- ½ cup mixed berries
- 2 tablespoons sliced almonds

Instructions:

1. Mix chia seeds, almond milk, vanilla, and honey. Let sit overnight.
2. Stir and top with mixed berries and sliced almonds.

Greek Yogurt and Honey Granola Bowl

Ingredients:

- 1 cup Greek yogurt
- ¼ cup granola
- 1 tablespoon honey
- ½ cup fresh berries

Instructions:

1. Spoon Greek yogurt into a bowl.
2. Top with granola, honey, and berries.

Quinoa and Fresh Fruit Bowl

Ingredients:

- ½ cup cooked quinoa
- ½ cup almond milk
- 1 teaspoon honey
- ½ cup mixed fruit (mango, berries, kiwi)
- 1 tablespoon chopped nuts

Instructions:

1. Mix cooked quinoa with almond milk and honey.
2. Top with fresh fruit and chopped nuts.

Green Detox Smoothie Bowl

Ingredients:

- 1 frozen banana
- 1 cup spinach
- ½ avocado
- ½ cup almond milk
- 1 teaspoon chia seeds
- Fresh fruit, coconut flakes, and granola for topping

Instructions:

1. Blend banana, spinach, avocado, almond milk, and chia seeds until smooth.
2. Pour into a bowl and top with fruit, coconut flakes, and granola.

Apple Cinnamon Oatmeal Bowl

Ingredients:

- ½ cup rolled oats
- 1 cup almond milk
- ½ apple, diced
- ½ teaspoon cinnamon
- 1 teaspoon maple syrup
- 1 tablespoon chopped walnuts

Instructions:

1. Cook oats in almond milk until creamy.
2. Stir in cinnamon and top with apple, maple syrup, and walnuts.

Tropical Mango Coconut Bowl

Ingredients:

- 1 frozen banana
- ½ cup frozen mango
- ½ cup coconut milk
- 1 tablespoon shredded coconut
- Fresh mango, kiwi, and granola for topping

Instructions:

1. Blend banana, mango, and coconut milk until smooth.
2. Pour into a bowl and top with shredded coconut, mango, kiwi, and granola.

Protein-Packed Egg and Avocado Bowl

Ingredients:

- 2 hard-boiled eggs, sliced
- ½ avocado, mashed
- 1 cup spinach
- ½ cup cooked quinoa
- 1 teaspoon olive oil
- Salt and pepper to taste

Instructions:

1. Arrange quinoa, eggs, and spinach in a bowl.
2. Add mashed avocado, drizzle with olive oil, and season with salt and pepper.

Choco-Banana Smoothie Bowl

Ingredients:

- 1 frozen banana
- 1 tablespoon cocoa powder
- ½ cup almond milk
- 1 teaspoon peanut butter
- 1 tablespoon dark chocolate chips
- Granola and sliced banana for topping

Instructions:

1. Blend banana, cocoa powder, almond milk, and peanut butter until smooth.
2. Pour into a bowl and top with chocolate chips, granola, and banana slices.

Spiced Pumpkin Oatmeal Bowl

Ingredients:

- ½ cup rolled oats
- 1 cup almond milk
- ¼ cup pumpkin purée
- ½ teaspoon cinnamon
- 1 teaspoon maple syrup
- 1 tablespoon pumpkin seeds

Instructions:

1. Cook oats in almond milk until creamy.
2. Stir in pumpkin purée, cinnamon, and maple syrup.
3. Top with pumpkin seeds.

Matcha and Coconut Yogurt Bowl

Ingredients:

- 1 cup coconut yogurt
- 1 teaspoon matcha powder
- 1 tablespoon honey
- ½ cup granola
- ½ banana, sliced
- 1 tablespoon shredded coconut

Instructions:

1. Mix matcha powder into coconut yogurt until smooth.
2. Spoon into a bowl and drizzle with honey.
3. Top with granola, banana slices, and shredded coconut.

Blueberry Walnut Overnight Oats Bowl

Ingredients:

- ½ cup rolled oats
- 1 cup almond milk
- 1 tablespoon chia seeds
- ½ teaspoon cinnamon
- ½ cup fresh blueberries
- 2 tablespoons chopped walnuts

Instructions:

1. Mix oats, almond milk, chia seeds, and cinnamon in a jar.
2. Refrigerate overnight.
3. In the morning, top with blueberries and walnuts.

Avocado and Smoked Salmon Quinoa Bowl

Ingredients:

- ½ cup cooked quinoa
- ½ avocado, sliced
- 3 ounces smoked salmon
- 1 tablespoon capers
- 1 teaspoon lemon juice
- 1 teaspoon olive oil
- Salt and pepper to taste

Instructions:

1. Arrange quinoa in a bowl.
2. Top with avocado, smoked salmon, and capers.
3. Drizzle with lemon juice and olive oil. Season with salt and pepper.

Chia and Flaxseed Superfood Bowl

Ingredients:

- ¼ cup chia seeds
- 1 cup almond milk
- 1 tablespoon ground flaxseeds
- ½ teaspoon vanilla extract
- 1 teaspoon honey
- Fresh berries and nuts for topping

Instructions:

1. Mix chia seeds, almond milk, flaxseeds, vanilla, and honey.
2. Refrigerate overnight until thick.
3. Stir and top with fresh berries and nuts.

Sweet Potato and Almond Butter Bowl

Ingredients:

- ½ cup mashed roasted sweet potato
- 1 tablespoon almond butter
- ½ teaspoon cinnamon
- 1 teaspoon maple syrup
- 1 tablespoon chopped almonds

Instructions:

1. Mix mashed sweet potato with almond butter, cinnamon, and maple syrup.
2. Spoon into a bowl and top with chopped almonds.

Strawberry and Cacao Nib Yogurt Bowl

Ingredients:

- 1 cup Greek yogurt
- ½ cup sliced strawberries
- 1 tablespoon cacao nibs
- 1 teaspoon honey
- 2 tablespoons granola

Instructions:

1. Spoon yogurt into a bowl.
2. Top with strawberries, cacao nibs, and granola.
3. Drizzle with honey.

Peanut Butter Chocolate Oatmeal Bowl

Ingredients:

- ½ cup rolled oats
- 1 cup almond milk
- 1 tablespoon cocoa powder
- 1 tablespoon peanut butter
- 1 teaspoon honey
- 1 tablespoon dark chocolate chips

Instructions:

1. Cook oats in almond milk until creamy.
2. Stir in cocoa powder, peanut butter, and honey.
3. Top with dark chocolate chips.

Spiced Pear and Pecan Quinoa Bowl

Ingredients:

- ½ cup cooked quinoa
- ½ pear, diced
- ½ teaspoon cinnamon
- 1 teaspoon maple syrup
- 2 tablespoons chopped pecans

Instructions:

1. Mix quinoa, cinnamon, and maple syrup.
2. Top with diced pear and pecans.

Mediterranean Feta and Chickpea Bowl

Ingredients:

- ½ cup cooked chickpeas
- ¼ cup crumbled feta cheese
- ½ cup cherry tomatoes, halved
- ¼ cucumber, diced
- 1 teaspoon olive oil
- 1 teaspoon lemon juice
- 1 teaspoon fresh parsley, chopped

Instructions:

1. Combine chickpeas, feta, tomatoes, and cucumber in a bowl.
2. Drizzle with olive oil and lemon juice.
3. Sprinkle with fresh parsley.

Carrot Cake Overnight Oats Bowl

Ingredients:

- ½ cup rolled oats
- 1 cup almond milk
- ½ cup grated carrot
- 1 tablespoon chia seeds
- ½ teaspoon cinnamon
- 1 teaspoon maple syrup
- 2 tablespoons chopped walnuts
- 1 tablespoon raisins

Instructions:

1. Mix oats, almond milk, grated carrot, chia seeds, cinnamon, and maple syrup in a jar.
2. Refrigerate overnight.
3. Stir and top with walnuts and raisins before serving.

Vanilla Bean and Berry Chia Bowl

Ingredients:

- ¼ cup chia seeds
- 1 cup almond milk
- 1 teaspoon vanilla bean paste
- 1 tablespoon honey
- ½ cup mixed berries
- 1 tablespoon sliced almonds

Instructions:

1. Mix chia seeds, almond milk, vanilla bean paste, and honey.
2. Refrigerate overnight until thick.
3. Stir and top with berries and almonds.

Dragon Fruit and Pineapple Bowl

Ingredients:

- ½ cup frozen dragon fruit
- ½ cup frozen pineapple
- ½ frozen banana
- ½ cup coconut milk
- 1 tablespoon shredded coconut
- 1 teaspoon chia seeds

Instructions:

1. Blend dragon fruit, pineapple, banana, and coconut milk until smooth.
2. Pour into a bowl and top with shredded coconut and chia seeds.

Scrambled Tofu and Avocado Bowl

Ingredients:

- ½ cup firm tofu, crumbled
- ½ teaspoon turmeric
- ½ teaspoon garlic powder
- Salt and pepper to taste
- ½ avocado, sliced
- 1 teaspoon olive oil
- ½ cup baby spinach

Instructions:

1. Sauté crumbled tofu with turmeric, garlic powder, salt, and pepper in olive oil.
2. Serve with avocado slices and baby spinach.

Almond Joy Smoothie Bowl

Ingredients:

- 1 frozen banana
- 1 tablespoon cocoa powder
- ½ cup coconut milk
- 1 tablespoon almond butter
- 1 tablespoon shredded coconut
- 1 tablespoon dark chocolate chips

Instructions:

1. Blend banana, cocoa powder, coconut milk, and almond butter until smooth.
2. Pour into a bowl and top with shredded coconut and dark chocolate chips.

Honeydew and Kiwi Yogurt Bowl

Ingredients:

- 1 cup Greek yogurt
- ½ cup honeydew melon, diced
- 1 kiwi, sliced
- 1 teaspoon honey
- 1 tablespoon granola

Instructions:

1. Spoon Greek yogurt into a bowl.
2. Top with honeydew, kiwi, and granola.
3. Drizzle with honey.

High-Protein Cottage Cheese Bowl

Ingredients:

- 1 cup cottage cheese
- ½ cup mixed berries
- 1 tablespoon chopped almonds
- 1 teaspoon flaxseeds
- 1 teaspoon honey

Instructions:

1. Spoon cottage cheese into a bowl.
2. Top with berries, almonds, and flaxseeds.
3. Drizzle with honey.

Cinnamon Apple Quinoa Porridge Bowl

Ingredients:

- ½ cup cooked quinoa
- 1 cup almond milk
- ½ apple, diced
- ½ teaspoon cinnamon
- 1 teaspoon maple syrup
- 1 tablespoon chopped pecans

Instructions:

1. Heat quinoa with almond milk, cinnamon, and maple syrup.
2. Top with diced apple and pecans.

Chocolate Hazelnut Smoothie Bowl

Ingredients:

- 1 frozen banana
- 1 tablespoon cocoa powder
- ½ cup almond milk
- 1 tablespoon hazelnut butter
- 1 teaspoon honey
- 1 tablespoon crushed hazelnuts

Instructions:

1. Blend banana, cocoa powder, almond milk, hazelnut butter, and honey until smooth.
2. Pour into a bowl and top with crushed hazelnuts.

Roasted Chickpea and Spinach Bowl

Ingredients:

- ½ cup roasted chickpeas
- ½ cup baby spinach
- 1 tablespoon tahini
- 1 teaspoon lemon juice
- 1 teaspoon olive oil
- Salt and pepper to taste

Instructions:

1. Toss roasted chickpeas with spinach, tahini, lemon juice, and olive oil.
2. Season with salt and pepper.

Blackberry and Mint Greek Yogurt Bowl

Ingredients:

- 1 cup Greek yogurt
- ½ cup blackberries
- 1 teaspoon honey
- 1 tablespoon chopped fresh mint
- 1 tablespoon granola

Instructions:

1. Spoon Greek yogurt into a bowl.
2. Top with blackberries, honey, mint, and granola.

Spicy Black Bean and Avocado Bowl

Ingredients:

- ½ cup cooked black beans
- ½ avocado, sliced
- ¼ cup cherry tomatoes, halved
- 1 teaspoon lime juice
- ½ teaspoon chili powder
- 1 teaspoon olive oil
- Fresh cilantro for garnish

Instructions:

1. Toss black beans with lime juice, chili powder, and olive oil.
2. Arrange in a bowl with avocado and cherry tomatoes.
3. Garnish with cilantro.

Caramelized Banana and Walnut Oat Bowl

Ingredients:

- ½ cup rolled oats
- 1 cup almond milk
- 1 banana, sliced
- 1 tablespoon butter
- 1 tablespoon brown sugar
- 2 tablespoons chopped walnuts
- ½ teaspoon cinnamon

Instructions:

1. Cook oats in almond milk until creamy.
2. In a pan, melt butter and brown sugar, then caramelize banana slices.
3. Spoon oats into a bowl and top with caramelized bananas, walnuts, and cinnamon.

Lemon Poppy Seed Chia Pudding Bowl

Ingredients:

- ¼ cup chia seeds
- 1 cup almond milk
- 1 teaspoon lemon zest
- 1 teaspoon honey
- 1 teaspoon poppy seeds
- Fresh berries for topping

Instructions:

1. Mix chia seeds, almond milk, lemon zest, honey, and poppy seeds.
2. Refrigerate overnight until thick.
3. Stir and top with fresh berries.

Maple Pecan Overnight Oats Bowl

Ingredients:

- ½ cup rolled oats
- 1 cup almond milk
- 1 teaspoon maple syrup
- ½ teaspoon cinnamon
- 2 tablespoons chopped pecans

Instructions:

1. Mix oats, almond milk, maple syrup, and cinnamon in a jar.
2. Refrigerate overnight.
3. Stir and top with chopped pecans before serving.

Spiced Chai Quinoa Bowl

Ingredients:

- ½ cup cooked quinoa
- 1 cup almond milk
- ½ teaspoon cinnamon
- ¼ teaspoon cardamom
- ¼ teaspoon nutmeg
- 1 teaspoon honey
- 1 tablespoon chopped almonds

Instructions:

1. Heat quinoa with almond milk, cinnamon, cardamom, nutmeg, and honey.
2. Spoon into a bowl and top with chopped almonds.

Raspberry and Dark Chocolate Yogurt Bowl

Ingredients:

- 1 cup Greek yogurt
- ½ cup raspberries
- 1 tablespoon dark chocolate shavings
- 1 teaspoon honey

Instructions:

1. Spoon yogurt into a bowl.
2. Top with raspberries, dark chocolate shavings, and honey.

Baked Oatmeal Blueberry Bowl

Ingredients:

- ½ cup rolled oats
- ½ teaspoon baking powder
- ½ teaspoon cinnamon
- 1 tablespoon maple syrup
- ½ cup almond milk
- ¼ cup blueberries

Instructions:

1. Mix oats, baking powder, cinnamon, maple syrup, and almond milk.
2. Fold in blueberries.
3. Bake at 350°F (175°C) for 20 minutes.

Fig and Almond Butter Smoothie Bowl

Ingredients:

- 1 frozen banana
- 2 fresh figs
- ½ cup almond milk
- 1 tablespoon almond butter
- 1 teaspoon honey
- 1 tablespoon sliced almonds

Instructions:

1. Blend banana, figs, almond milk, almond butter, and honey until smooth.
2. Pour into a bowl and top with sliced almonds.

Banana Nut Muffin Oatmeal Bowl

Ingredients:

- ½ cup rolled oats
- 1 cup almond milk
- 1 banana, mashed
- ½ teaspoon cinnamon
- 1 tablespoon chopped walnuts
- 1 teaspoon maple syrup

Instructions:

1. Cook oats in almond milk until creamy.
2. Stir in mashed banana and cinnamon.
3. Top with walnuts and maple syrup.

Hemp and Coconut Yogurt Bowl

Ingredients:

- 1 cup coconut yogurt
- 1 tablespoon hemp seeds
- 1 teaspoon honey
- ½ cup fresh berries
- 1 tablespoon shredded coconut

Instructions:

1. Spoon coconut yogurt into a bowl.
2. Top with hemp seeds, honey, berries, and shredded coconut.

Golden Turmeric Chia Pudding Bowl

Ingredients:

- ¼ cup chia seeds
- 1 cup almond milk
- ½ teaspoon turmeric powder
- ½ teaspoon cinnamon
- 1 teaspoon honey
- 1 tablespoon shredded coconut
- Fresh berries for topping

Instructions:

1. Mix chia seeds, almond milk, turmeric, cinnamon, and honey.
2. Refrigerate overnight until thick.
3. Stir and top with shredded coconut and fresh berries.

Pear and Cinnamon Greek Yogurt Bowl

Ingredients:

- 1 cup Greek yogurt
- ½ pear, sliced
- ½ teaspoon cinnamon
- 1 teaspoon honey
- 1 tablespoon granola
- 1 tablespoon chopped walnuts

Instructions:

1. Spoon Greek yogurt into a bowl.
2. Top with pear slices, cinnamon, honey, granola, and walnuts.

Pomegranate and Pistachio Bowl

Ingredients:

- 1 cup coconut yogurt
- ½ cup pomegranate seeds
- 2 tablespoons crushed pistachios
- 1 teaspoon maple syrup

Instructions:

1. Spoon yogurt into a bowl.
2. Top with pomegranate seeds, pistachios, and drizzle with maple syrup.

Dark Cherry Almond Butter Bowl

Ingredients:

- 1 frozen banana
- ½ cup frozen dark cherries
- ½ cup almond milk
- 1 tablespoon almond butter
- 1 teaspoon cacao nibs

Instructions:

1. Blend banana, dark cherries, almond milk, and almond butter until smooth.
2. Pour into a bowl and top with cacao nibs.

Pumpkin Spice Smoothie Bowl

Ingredients:

- ½ frozen banana
- ½ cup pumpkin purée
- ½ cup almond milk
- ½ teaspoon cinnamon
- ¼ teaspoon nutmeg
- 1 tablespoon granola
- 1 teaspoon pumpkin seeds

Instructions:

1. Blend banana, pumpkin purée, almond milk, cinnamon, and nutmeg until smooth.
2. Pour into a bowl and top with granola and pumpkin seeds.

Sweet and Savory Avocado Egg Bowl

Ingredients:

- ½ avocado, mashed
- 2 soft-boiled eggs, halved
- ½ cup cooked quinoa
- 1 teaspoon olive oil
- Salt and pepper to taste
- 1 teaspoon hot sauce (optional)

Instructions:

1. Place mashed avocado in a bowl.
2. Add quinoa and top with soft-boiled eggs.
3. Drizzle with olive oil, season with salt and pepper, and add hot sauce if desired.

Cashew Butter and Cacao Smoothie Bowl

Ingredients:

- 1 frozen banana
- ½ cup almond milk
- 1 tablespoon cashew butter
- 1 teaspoon cacao powder
- 1 teaspoon honey
- 1 tablespoon crushed cashews

Instructions:

1. Blend banana, almond milk, cashew butter, cacao powder, and honey until smooth.
2. Pour into a bowl and top with crushed cashews.

Gingerbread Oatmeal Bowl

Ingredients:

- ½ cup rolled oats
- 1 cup almond milk
- ½ teaspoon cinnamon
- ½ teaspoon ground ginger
- 1 teaspoon molasses
- 1 tablespoon chopped pecans

Instructions:

1. Cook oats in almond milk until creamy.
2. Stir in cinnamon, ginger, and molasses.
3. Top with chopped pecans.

Mocha Banana Protein Bowl

Ingredients:

- 1 frozen banana
- ½ cup almond milk
- 1 teaspoon instant coffee or espresso powder
- 1 tablespoon cocoa powder
- 1 scoop chocolate protein powder
- 1 teaspoon honey
- 1 tablespoon dark chocolate shavings

Instructions:

1. Blend banana, almond milk, coffee, cocoa powder, protein powder, and honey until smooth.
2. Pour into a bowl and top with dark chocolate shavings.

www.ingramcontent.com/pod-product-compliance
Lightning Source LLC
LaVergne TN
LVHW081332060526
838201LV00055B/2591